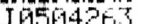

I0504263

Crushing it With YouTube!

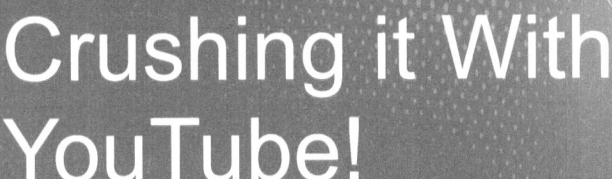

→ Taking Your YouTube Business to the Next Level

Contents

Introduction

In the past few years we have witnessed a revolution in our social lives; everything is online from our business to our pass time activities. More and more businesses are making it a priority to have a strong online presence simply because there is plenty of money in the online business. If you are reading this then it is safe to say you are also looking to have your slice of this online pie.

As a marketer having and maintaining an online presence that is not only strong but reputable is supposed to be one of your top priorities if not the most important priority. There are so many ways that one can this, so many technical terms such as the ubiquitous Search Engine Optimization (SEO) and it is easy for you to be bogged down with this and forget about all else. Well, this is not in any way meant to downplay the importance of SEO; it is actually very brilliant in itself. However, it is quite easy for marketers to overlook the second largest search engine available on the internet; YouTube.

The Importance of s Strong Presence

At this point I am sure that there is a modicum of skepticism in you that is telling you that YouTube is not all that important because it is only a *video* search engine. Well, sorry to inform you that you are wrong because it is important. Here are the reasons why YouTube counts:

- YouTube alone is significantly larger than other search engines such as Yahoo, Bing, Ask and AOL....*Put Together*
- In each and every month the YouTube Search engine receive approximately 3 billion searches
- On average for every 2 searches on the internet, there is 1 search that is on YouTube. That is 50 per cent of the searches!!
- YouTube is able to attract more adults aged 18-35 living in the US than any other cable network in the market
- In each and every month, there are approximately 6 billion hours that are spent on YouTube alone.

This is just the tip of the iceberg on all the mind boggling statistics concerning YouTube. In the event that you are not interested in having a slice of this lucrative pie, then there is a chance that your marketing campaign has the bar set a tad bit too low.

Breaking Down a YouTube Video

Let us begin with a rhetorical question. When is the last time you took time off your busy schedule and logged in to YouTube to engage yourself in a few minutes of watching a self-promotional video that was poorly produces, boring and at the end of it all it was not meant to help you to achieve anything?

Well, no need to answer that one. Nobody has time for such self-punishment.

There are few reasons as to why people will visit YouTube and they are very simple:

1. They are faced with a specific problem and they need to find a quick answer to it.
2. They are looking to pass time and enjoy a few entertaining videos of cats playing the piano or whatever tickles their fancy.

Being a professional business, you should always seek to offer the first option: **a solution to a problem.** As a rule of thumb you should always steer clear of self-promotional videos. However, there is an exception for when you are aiming for a pre-roll advertising but that shall be covered later in the article. Your bread and butter should always be answers to specific problems or videos that are beneficial to the watchers in that they will walk away having gained some bit of information.

If you are looking to launch a video marketing campaign on this YouTube platform then there are just but 3 essential steps that you need to be aware of.

1. Launching a Platform
2. Creating and Producing the right Video Content
3. Extensive YouTube SEO followed by Marketing

Launching a Platform

Let us begin with the first steps. You need to develop your platform through meticulous planning. This means that you need to come up with a strategy that is so sound that you will have no problem in risking a significant amount of your marketing funds on it. This may sound more daunting and formidable than it actually is; however, it is quite important.

The chief components of a successful video marketing strategy are as follows:

1. Identifying the key objectives of your campaign
2. Identifying the right target audience
3. Identifying the most appropriate type of video that you will produce

Identifying your Key Objectives

This is probably self-explanatory but for the sake of exhaustively covering all aspects there is need to cover this area. It is true for almost all aspects of life that if you do not have a clear cut objective then it follows that you do not know where you desire to go. Concomitantly, if you have no idea where it is you are going then there is no way that you will ever get there.

A chief component of planning is setting up goals that are SMART. This means that your goals need to be specific and significant. They also need to be measurable in that you can keep track of your progress. Your goals need to be agreed upon; ensure that all the stakeholders of the strategy have agreed on the objectives so as to ensure that they commit themselves to ensuring that it is achieved. They also need to be realistic or attainable; do not set objective that cannot be achieved such as to get 3 billion views in one night. Your goals also need to be time bound; set a goal that is supposed to be achieved within a specific time period.

If you follow these simple guidelines then there is a high likelihood that you shall never be disappointed.

For instructional purposes, let us consider an example of a company such as Globe Fastening Consultancy that may be looking into making a YouTube Video and the following will be the objectives.

1. **Create** an additional **2000visitors** to the company website with **5** months of specific video marketing

2. **Create** an additional revenue stream of approximately **$1,500** for every month within the first **6** months of the video marketing campaign

3. **Double** the overall number of clients within the first six months of video marketing.

Identifying your Target Audience

The rapid shift of consumer behavior to the various online platforms has meant that has become more important for you to identify the right target audiences for your marketing campaign. There is however an upside to this shift as it has become easier for you to gain knowledge about your potential client base. To add to the basic information such as their demographics and locations, it is possible to get a better understanding of the types of sites they have a preference for, the content that they are interested in, and much more. Clearly defining this target audience for your market can aid you in custom fitting content such as social media posts, photos, paid adverts, and videos. It can also help you in identifying the marketing methods that would have the most positive impact to your business.

Targeting the right audience is certainly beneficial in ensuring that you get the most out of your marketing dollars. In identifying the right target audience, you need to look into the 5 Ws: Who, What, When, Where and Why.

Who

Who are the current customers?

It is important to know who constitutes your current customer base. Given that they have already purchased from you in the past, you can make use of this information to get a better insight that will aid you in identifying the constitution of your core target audience. Here you can reach out to them via social media, email, or even within the store using a simple survey that will gather information concerning their interests, demographics, and their needs,. You can also capitalize on this opportunity to find out what the customers love most about your business and the products that they like the most.

Who do you want to purchase your products?

You also need to identify the audiences that you intend to target in order to aid you in the expansion of your customer base. However, it is vital that you are realistic in considering who will actually purchase your products. For instance, if the current customer base of your high end boutique shop is majorly comprised of college students and teens that are fashion conscious, then it would be realistic to consider expanding your customer base to young professional women. However, it would be far-fetched to consider moms that are budget conscious.

Who are you currently marketing to?

If the focus of your targeted online marketing is a specific demographic that you are interested in then ensure that you keep track of the results in order to see the performance of your efforts. For example, you may begin by tracking phone calls just to get an insight as to how well your marketing is doing. If you get a positive result, continue to focus on these groups. If however they are not working consider solutions to these problems and tweak your message as well as strategy. Another positive that may come from monitoring your results is that you may reveal an audience that you had not been exclusively targeting. For instance, if your search advertising is resulting in more conversations over the phone than via desktop, then you may need to consider your mobile presence by designing an optimized mobile landing site in order to create a smart mobile experience for your mobile customers.

What

What is the background of your customers?

This is arguably one of the most important questions that you should ask yourself when you are defining your target audience. If you are able to identify attributes such as age, gender, education level, hobbies, geographic location, income level, interests, family status, and much more then it will help you in determining the kind of online advertising that you need to make use of in order to reach the right customers for your business.

What do they purchase?

Try to seek to know whether your customers purchase more of a certain item or are interested in one service. If you are able to identify the products that are your best sellers, you will in a better position to not only make smarter inventory choices but also in tailoring your message so as to reach as many customers who are interested in these items. Additionally, by closely monitoring review sites and social media, you can always keep abreast of what the customer's think of your service; if it is good then you can maintain the standards and it is not then you get a chance to change.

When

When are your products bought?

Try and identify whether your customers purchase your products at a specific time during the year or whether they are purchasing throughout the year. By understanding the seasonality or the frequency of your business, you can be able to create messages that will target the customers during the right time in the cycle. For instance, a plumber is often sought out whenever the need arises, therefore optimizing search ads and content for his plumbing services may be of help in targeting consumers that are looking for an on the spot purchasing decision. However, a customer that is looking to purchase a new car has a higher likelihood of researching on dealers, vehicles, reviews, and offers on a number of different sites for a stretched duration of time. Ergo, it is vital that you take the length of time of your normal buying cycle into account.

When do the customers currently interact with your brand?

Ensuring that you target the right audience is not only crucial for gaining new sales but also for developing your online brand. For example, by monitoring the times when the fans interact with your posts on social media you can be in a better position of planning a schedule of when to post some content so as to get the optimum visibility as well as engagement. Here, let us imagine that your brand gets more traction on Fridays as compared to Mondays then you should take advantage of this knowledge to post content that is engaging or promotions and special offers for the followers and fans when they are most likely to see the content.

Where

Where are your customers located?

Defining the exact location of your current customers can be of significant help in terms of concentrating your target marketing efforts. By making use of geographic targeting in display and search advertising you can be able to create lead that are optimized through displaying your message only to audience that are in your service area. For instance, if you are a Dentist in your local town then there is a very low likelihood that you are going to receive a client from a different State or country through your adverts. Therefore, in order to target the right consumers for your products, you need to make use of the appropriate keywords, such as location-specific phases, within your content in order to improve the overall chance of them showing up when the customers such for businesses similar to yours in the directories or search engines.

Where did your customers find you online?

A very easy and effective way of identifying your target audience is in finding out where your customers presently first found out about your business. Whether it is from the local directories, search engines, social media, word of mouth, or online reviews, by knowing where they first found out about your business can aid you in planning where to concentrate your targeting efforts.

Why

Why do they purchase?

Ideally, a majority of the purchases can be grouped into two: needs and wants. By understanding your key products and services as well as the reasons why customers choose to purchase them can offer you with further insight into your target audience and the process they go through in finding your business. For example, a customer that is seeking the services of a plumber will have considerably different expectations as well as a journey compared to another customer that is looking for a spa. Ergo, in understanding the why behind the purchase, you are in a better position of determining the most probable path of purchase.

Why do customers purchase from your competitors?

With the highly competitive markets today, customers are often spoiled for choice when it comes to purchasing. Therefore, there are numerous reasons as to why customers may opt to buy their goods from your competitors. It may be the case that your competitors have a superior customer service, they are more engaging with their customers or their followers and fans online, offer appealing discounts, have a better reputation, or their content is better optimized such that the customers can find them easily when they search. Therefore, if you can clearly understand why they prefer to buy from your competitors and not from you may aid you in tailoring your approach in order for you to reach them and convert them to being your customers.

Answering all these questions is quite crucial in identifying the target audience for your customers. Studies have shown that the average consumers will make use of more than 10 sources of information before they make a decision on purchasing a product. This makes it even more critical that you need to identify your target audience in order to build a marketing plan that is able to reach your desired target audience where they are most likely to see it and engage with it.

Identify The Right Content

There are very many different types of videos on YouTube that are available. Honestly, you can find almost anything on YouTube. Here are some of the most popular kinds of videos that you are likely to encounter:

1. **Educational Videos:** these are basically recordings or videos of public sessions that are conducted in lectures or auditoriums, or sometimes an individual just standing and talking may suffice (he may be standing illustrating his content with a white board or other visual materials. It is important to note that sometimes this tactic may be a tad bit consuming with respect to time, however it is quite cheap to produce in comparison to other kinds of videos.

2. **Webinars:** these will normally be characterized with some Power Point Presentations with a few graphics accompanied with a voice over on it. These are also very popular and they are quite easy and fast to produce. In terms of cost, they are very cheap and effective provided you have the basic skills required.

3. **Tutorials:** These can be defined as videos that are elaborate and dynamic in structure. These videos can either be animated or they can clearly show the process that one must take in order to perform a certain task. For instance, how to repair a car. Characteristically these types of videos are time consuming and often expensive.

The third kind of video is what you should probably look into producing. Admittedly, they are both costly and a tad bit difficult to produce which may put you off. However, these elaborate tutorials are generally the most appreciated kinds of videos online. With these characteristic, it has the highest potential of generating traffic as well as exposure to your site.

However, just because it is the most appreciated does not necessarily mean it is the best fit for your business. Once you have understood your target audience, you will be in a better position of understanding the kind of video that they are most likely to respond well to and then you can make use of the above information and capitalize on it.

Making a decision on the right kind of video for you to produce will help you significantly when it comes to making your budget. It is important to remember that as you are creating your budget; your objectives should always be a key concern. You would not be realistic if you were expecting that your videos would drive a seven figure revenue stream whilst working with a three figure budget.

Producing the right Video Content

This is where the exciting action begins, when you finally get to produce the videos to post on YouTube. Likewise, as the excitement begins so does the rise in cost of video marketing.

Much like the aforementioned planning stage, there are three different stages that one must go through in order to produce an appropriate video content. These are as follows:

1. Buying the right kind of equipment
2. Identifying video topics
3. Filming the video

Buying the Right kind of Equipment

Regardless of the type of video marketing that you are considering, you cannot escape some form of investment for it. Here, you will most certainly be required to spend on the purchase of some equipment. This is particularly the case for some kinds of videos as they are more sensitive to quality.

Let us take a scenario that the hypothetical company that we had earlier discussed is deciding to make use of in-depth tutorials. This will be quite appropriate for their desired target audience as they have thoroughly researched online and made findings that there are many individuals that are very interested in Do It Yourself Gasket replacement videos, or something like that.

Globe Fasteners Consultancy will be faced with a choice of spending some significant amount of money on a number of items:

- A quality professional video camera. This will probably set them back a high 3 figure or mid four figures. Quality videos will be important so they cannot avoid this cost.
- A standard tripod. This would as well set them back low three figures.
- A quality video editing software. There are a number of free online software that are free to use but these often have restrictions and most often than not will have watermarks on them. Again, this will set them back mid three figures.
- A standard wireless microphone. These are not very expensive and will go for about three figures.
- Lighting equipment. A good video must have quality lighting lest you have dark spots in the video which tend to be frustrating to watch. The cost of this will vary from mid two figures to high three figures.
- So much more

At this point it is important to remind you that video marketing may not be the most cost effective kind of marketing that you can think of. In fact, there are a number of cases where the marketing campaign can go belly up and run losses. Therefore, before you hop on this bandwagon, you might need to take time to ensure that you have the necessary funds as well as the time to invest in this kind of project.

Finding Appropriate Topics for Videos

Making videos is very reliant on creativity and innovation. If your agenda is to be prolific in terms of producing videos then you should not be surprised that you will likely run out of ideas quite fast. This is especially the case if you are dealing with a niche product such as the replacement of gaskets or windows. Let us be honest, there are only so many ways in which you can make a video about the aforementioned topics before they start to recycle.

In the event that you find yourself stuck in the same kind of predicament, there are a number of avenues that you can explore that will help you in generating new ideas for your videos?

Recycle a blog post that you posted a long time ago. You can locate one of your first blog posts and do your best to rework it such that you come up with a tutorial or appropriate video. For instance, if you have in the past worked in extensive guides on how to do things such as web hosting, you can now endeavor to make a video from this.

"Borrow" an idea from a competitor. This may sound like some under handed tactics and probably even illegal, however, you should know that it is not actually against the law to do so. After all, there is nothing that is new under the sun. But it would be wise to mention that this does not mean that you should actually steal the actual video that was posted by your competitor. Now that would be illegal! What we are suggesting that you can review what the competitor is posting and with this you can be able to see what is currently trending in the market and then find out the topics that would best resonate with your audience thus resulting in more traffic.

Once you have done this, you are only required to come up with a better video and market it in a more efficient manner as compared to the competitor.

Make use of Uber Suggest to come up with a comprehensive list of appropriate keywords. This tool is quite effective and comes highly recommended. An apt comparison would be Google Instant that is hopped up on steroids. What you get from Uber Suggest is a tool that is web-based and allows you to insert a specific key word and it will instantly churn out hundreds of new key words that you can use. This is the ultimate tool in the event that you need to brainstorm on keywords.

Consult your audience: There is no better way of coming up with topics for new videos like to ask the people who actually want to watch them. Your audience can provide you with an invaluable source of video topics whenever you feel like you are in a rut for new ideas by simply asking them. Come up with a survey which can easily be created with the help of free tools such as Survey Monkey and then consult some of your previous customers and request them to participate in the survey.

It is not always the case that you will be lost for ideas for a video topic, there are some niches such as WordPress how to and conversion rate optimization, where there will always be an overabundance of ideas for videos. Your brain will be literally buzzing with ideas for videos.

If you find yourself in such a case where you have an oversupply of ideas for your video then it would be wise to remember that you need to clearly vet the profitability and feasibility of each and every idea.

What this means is that while there are many ideas for video topics, not all of them will be worth the effort and cost. If you perceive that the chances for you to make any money on the ideas are slim or not existent entirely, or if the traffic that could be generated from the given topic is not justifiable, then there is absolutely no reason why It is not always the case that you will be lost for ideas for a video topic, there are some niches such as WordPress how to and conversion rate optimization, where there will always be an overabundance of ideas for videos. Your brain will be literally buzzing with ideas for videos.

If you find yourself in such a case where you have an oversupply of ideas for your video then it would be wise to remember that you need to clearly vet the profitability and feasibility of each and every idea.

What this means is that while there are many ideas for video topics, not all of them will be worth the effort and cost. If you perceive that the chances for you to make any money on the ideas are slim or not existent entirely, or if the traffic that could be generated from the given topic is not justifiable, then there is absolutely no reason why you need to invest up to four figures in creating such a video.

It is a waste of resources that would eventually earn you nothing. Do not waste your time on it!

Shooting of the Video

When you watch a video on YouTube it is very easy not to appreciate the kind of effort that goes into making such a video. There are a lot of behind the scene activities that are undertaken so that a successful and engaging video can be filmed.

To begin with, you absolutely need to have a script. This should not be just another slipshod script, it should be a good script that is capable of meeting your objectives. Failure to which, you run the risk of sounding like a complete idiot in front of all your viewers and the potential customers who will view your video.

Secondly, you are going to need an appropriate location where you are going to shoot your video. If you are shooting a video about fixing doors then there is a high likelihood that location will not be a major issue. All that you will need is a room that is well lit and a door that is in need of fixing, which is something that can be simulated in an easy way (all you would require is a door and an ample amount of force exerted with a shoulder and voila! You have a door than needs fixing for your video). However, if you were shooting a video for a Motor company then you may run into some bit of trouble as you would require a road that does not have traffic and is nice enough for your set up.

Finally, one of the most crucial things that you need to factor in when you are producing your video is that it needs to be engaging! Make sure you enunciate your words – the viewers should be able to hear you without any difficulty. Remember if you are making the video then you are communicating and communication is a performance art. Ergo, you need to make sure you entertain your audience. Do not hesitate to throw in a joke or two provided they are appropriate and in good taste. Admittedly, when you are making a video about fixing a door or a radiator fan it is a rather somber affair and there is not much room for jokes, however, there is always going to be a chance where you can throw in a witty one liner in order to ensure that your audience is engaged and stimulated.

There is also another factor that you should always take into consideration when you are making the video; the *length* of the video. Let us be honest, there are very few people who are willing to sit through a 50 minute monster video on how to fix a door! There are only so few hours in a day and with the limited attention span of people in this digital age this is not practical. Admittedly, there it is not possible to fine a length that suits all video content; a pseudo sweet spot for length of videos. However, according to the findings of research that was conducted on a number of social media sites, it was noted most people would prefer a YouTube video that is less than 5 minutes; somewhere between a low four minute and a high three minute would be just right.

A number of analysts online conclude that a shorter video is always better. It is not beneficial to go overboard on the length of videos. Furthermore, a short video is often cheaper than a long video.

There is another vital aspect to shooting a video that you need to consider and that is the thumbnail to your video. Here, you have just but a couple of options. The first of which would be to create a custom thumbnail of your own choosing and the other alternative would be to upload the video as it is and let YouTube to pick out a random millisecond or two from your video to select as your thumbnail.

The smart option here would be to go with the former option given that you are going to rely on this thumbnail to attract your customers. The ideal thumbnail is one that has the following attributes:

- The thumbnail should be branded. This means that it should have your unique logo at the bottom left corner. The aim of this is to improve the overall visibility of the video.
- The thumbnail needs to be able to describe the topic of the video. Just by looking at it, a potential watcher needs to be able to have a slight clue as to what the video is about
- The thumbnail should be attractive such that it causes the watchers to want to click on it.

The trait that you want to dedicate a significant amount of time on is the last one: *causing people to want to click.* Let us take the example that you are making a video that is like a Power Point in style, then for a thumbnail you need to make a screenshot of the slide that contains the most helpful and informative content. By doing this, you will be able to let the viewer to know that they are going to get some useful information even before they watch the video and this will cause them to click on the video.

YouTube SEO

Awesome! You have successfully come up with a video marketing plan for the next three months. This is an excellent and engaging video that spans 3 minutes and 50 seconds filled with very captivating content, and you have successfully uploaded the video to YouTube.

Then what next?

You patiently wait for the views counter to start ticking away. At first nothing happens but you tell yourself it has only been 15 minutes so wait a little longer. 15 minutes turn into hours which turn into a day then days and still you have nothing to show for all your hard work except a dismal 10 views (and this is including yourself, your friends, and every member of the production team watching it from separate computers). At this point you are almost concluding that YouTube videos are not for you and the whole endeavor was a complete waste of time.

Hold on for a minute! There might be a simple reason as to why your video is performing dismally and it seems no one is interested in watching it. Could it be that you have completely forgotten about the **marketing** aspect of making the video?

Of Course it is!

It is important that you learn this concept early on, lest you get frustrated with online video marketing. Regardless of how captivating the content of your video is or how much you think it is beneficial to people, if people are unable to find your video, there is no way they are going to watch it, nor will you be able to make money off it. Therefore, you need to market your video and the first step of this process is through optimizing your video such that it gets higher rankings as compared to other videos in the SERPs.

Despite the fact that Google purchased YouTube a while back, the search engine for the video site still maintains its own unique algorithm. The implication of this is that whatever might be suitable for the SERPs on Google might not necessarily be suitable for YouTube.

The good news here is that the basic concepts are still the same therefore you do not need to learn any new skills in order to be able to pull this one off. These concepts encompass the following: ensure that you engage your visitors, and make sure that your video is very relevant to your basic key words. The four key stones for YouTube SEO are:

1. The relevancy of videos
2. The relevancy of your channel
3. The View Count
4. The View ratings and engagement

Relevancy of Videos

It is almost goes without saying that there is no way a YouTube spider can watch a video that you have posted and make a conclusion that the video is not relevant to a particular keyword (however, it would be quite exciting if it were able to do so).

Instead of actually watching your video, YouTube spiders perform a ranking of your video on the basis of what they are able to read this being the description of the video and its title.

These are similar to the meta descriptions and the headlines that are found in Google. All you need to do is to insert your keywords and your secondary key words and then tag your video in a manner that is appropriate.

Here is an example of a description and title that are optimized for our hypothetical company Globe Fasteners Consultancy:

How to Replace a Leaky Faucet in 5 Minutes

The following is step by step video guide that will show you how to replace a leaky faucet **(primary keyword)** *– know how to replace the faucet in five minutes. Equipment necessary: wrench, pliers, replacement faucet* **(these will now constitute the secondary keywords or the LSI).**

Here the key words were incorporated into the description of the video as well as the title. The impact of this is that now the spider will be able to know that the video that has been uploaded is relevant to the keyword "how to replace a leaky faucet".

Relevancy of the Channel

If you have any background information about SEO then you will be well aware that by simply just optimizing one solitary blog will not suffice! You entire website is required to be in good terms with Google for the keywords that are related for you to have any sort of traffic directed your way.

This is the same concept that applies for channel relevancy.

You need to make use of your channel description to compose a concise description that is rich in key words and clearly gives information about who you are and what it is that you do.

For instance:

Globe Fasteners Consultancy **(keyword)** *is a hardware supplier***(another keyword)** *that is well known and very respectable that is dedicated to making the process of replacing household fittings such as faucets, windows and doors a painless and affordable endeavor. We have been supplying household fitting to over 3000 customers for over 20 years.*

It is also quite crucial that you append a link to your website. The reason for this is that the link in your channel description is often designed as a follow. Also, you will get a helpful, no charge included backlink from a PR-9 website.

You should further ensure that your YouTube channel is only producing videos that have a relation to exclusively one niche – if you are thinking on uploading a video on riding bicycles on our Global Fastening Consultancy channel then DO NOT!

View Count

This area creates a conundrum much like the chicken and the egg one.

Conventionally one of the ways that YouTube videos are ranked is through view counts. However, it is very difficult for you to get views without already having a high ranking in SERPs.

A possible solution here is to market your videos extensively on social media, emails, blogs and anything platform that you have at your disposal.

VideoRatings

It is completely unacceptable if all your viewers are abandoning your videos 5 seconds after clicking on it. It is also very disheartening if a negligible percentage of your viewers are taking the time to leave a comment on your videos. Also, if your dislike to like ratio numbers read something like 50-50 then this is quite bad.

In the event that viewers do not engage with your video, then the YouTube spiders will automatically make the assumption that your video does not have the necessary quality and often this is the case.

Also having a high video view count, probably in five figures, is pointless if over half of those people are rushing down to leave negative comments or disliking you video.

One of the easiest ways that you can ensure there is an increase in the overall level of engagement in your videos in the form of shares, subscriptions, votes and comments is by simply requesting your visitors to do so. At the end of the video, simply ask them to engage in whatever manner that you prefer.

YouTube Advertising

There are a number of pre-roll ad options that are available to YouTube advertisers such as:

- In stream: these are those ads that come before, during or after a video.

- In-search: these are those ads that pop up on the search page

- In-display: these are those ads that pop up next to the YouTube videos.

Generally, the instream ads have been found to be the most engaging of all the above ads, the other two have been noted to result in banner blindness.

However, after the introduction of TrueView users have the option of skipping and ad after 5 seconds of watching it. The Advertisers will only pay for the ad if the users watch the ad for 30 seconds or the whole ad if it is shorter than 30 seconds.

An interesting fact is that the pre-roll ads are quite effective as over 30 per cent of YouTube users watch these ads. They also have a relatively high engagement, much higher than of those viewers who are forced to watch these ads in between the video.

Your video being very engaging, notwithstanding, the overall success with pre-roll advertising is dependent on a number of different factors. When you are developing a YouTube advertising campaign, it is important that you consider the following things:

- The kind of ad that is best suited for your niche

- Advertising via mobile

- Always make it engaging enough to make users watch past 5 seconds

Video Marketing

There is no argument that YouTube is the titan of video marketing, it is worth considering that there are other networks that can host your video as well. These include Vimeo, Viddler, Daily Motion, Facebook, and Hulu among many others.

These sites are capable of putting up impressive figures in terms of views in every month. Networks such as Daily Motion can put up views of hundreds of millions in every month. If you aggregate these figure with those of the other networks then you have numbers that are too high to ignore.

However, at this point you may be thinking of the cumbersome task of signing up to all the different sites and distributing the videos individually to each network and this may be a tad bit off putting.

However, thanks to an entrepreneur somewhere you have One Load that can do that for you.

OneLoad is a site that allows you to upload a video one time and it will distribute it to a whopping 18 different video networks at the same time. You may be required to part with some few dollars in the form of subscription fees but it is a worthwhile investment. There is of course the free plan that has limited features.

Conclusion

Video marketing is certainly not an easy, cheap and simple method of advertising, however, it does work otherwise the countless scores of businesses would not be doing it. While there are numerous ways that video advertising can be done online and through the internet, YouTube has revolutionized the way videos are shared and adverts made. Savvy users keen on making their presence or that of their products felt tap into the capability of YouTube.